# The E[ss]e[ntial]
# KNO[T BOOK]

# The Essential
# KNOT BOOK

## Knots, Bends, Hitches, Whippings & Splices

## Colin Jarman

### Third Edition

INTERNATIONAL MARINE / McGRAW-HILL
Camden, Maine • New York • Chicago • San Francisco • Lisbon
• London • Madrid • Mexico City • Milan • New Delhi • San Juan
• Seoul • Singapore • Sydney • Toronto

# The *McGraw·Hill* Companies

2 3 4 5 6 7 8 9 IMP/IMP 0 9 8 7 6 5 4

This edition published 2004 by International Marine,
a division of The McGraw-Hill Companies.

First published in Great Britain by Adlard Coles Ltd 1984.
Third edition published in Great Britain by Adlard Coles Ltd 2003.

Printed and bound in Singapore by Tien Wah Ltd.

A CIP catalog record for this book is available from the Library of Congress.

ISBN 0-07-143237-X

*Acknowledgments:*
The author would like to thank both English Braids Ltd and Marlow Ropes Ltd
for their help with the production of this book

# Contents

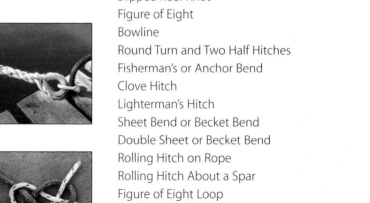

## 2 Whippings                                   49

## 3 Splicing                                    55

# Some Rope Terms Explained

**Bight** The middle of a line or, more commonly, a curve or loop taken in a line well away from either end.

**Bitter end** The end of a line, rope or wire.

**Core** Centre of rope. Modern ropes have separately constructed core and covering (sheath).

**Core strand** (heart strand). Straight strand running through centre (core, heart) of wire rope.

**Fall** End of halyard that is handled, winched and cleated.

**Fibres** Smallest part of rope made collectively into yarns which are in turn made up into strands that are then used to form the whole rope.

**Frapping turns** Turns of rope binding things together.

**Heart strand** (core strand). Straight strand running through centre of wire rope.

**Lay** The 'twist' pattern of a three strand rope.

**Lay up** Twist strands together to form a rope.

**Marry** Interweave unlayed strands prior to splicing together.

**Milk** The sheath of a rope is slipped down over a splice by 'milking' it.

**Round turn** A rope's end makes a round turn on something when it passes right around it through 540 degrees to enclose the object and point back parallel to its own standing part.

**Serve** Cover over either with tight binding of light twine or, more commonly nowadays, adhesive tape.

**Sheath** The outside cover of a plaited 'core and sheath' rope.

**Standing part** The main, non-working part of a line.

**Stop, to** To lash, seize or tape over temporarily, usually to prevent unlaying.

**Strand** Constituent part of rope. First subdivision, eg three strand laid rope.

**Thimble** Plastic or metal shaped eye inserted into spliced eye.

*Three-strand*

*Multiplait*

*Sixteen-plait with three-strand core*

*Braided with braided core*

**Throat** Point at which two parts of rope re-unite after passing round thimble or forming soft eye.

**Tuck, to** Weave ends of strands into laid up rope to make splice.

**Unlay, to** Open up and separate strands of laid rope or unravel plaited rope.

**Whip, to** Bind rope's end to prevent unlaying.

**Whipping** Binding on rope's end preventing unlaying.

**Worm** Spiral along groove between strands of laid rope.

**Yarns** Fibres are twisted together to form yarns, which are in turn used to make up strands forming rope.

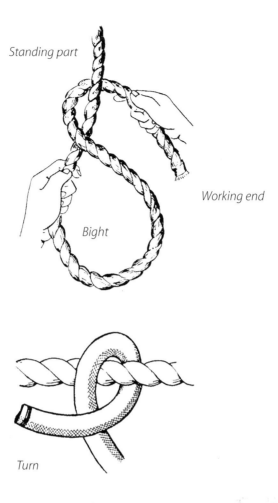

*Standing part*

*Working end*

*Bight*

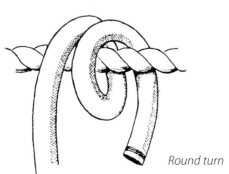

*Turn*

*Round turn*

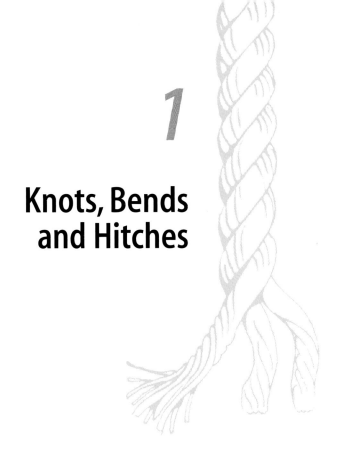

# 1

# Knots, Bends and Hitches

# Reef Knot

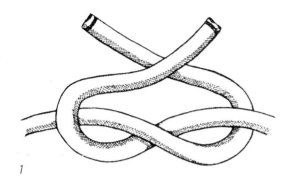

1

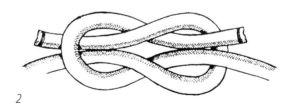

2

Originally used to tie off the ends of reef points when shortening sail, this symmetrical, flat knot can be formed with load on both standing parts and can also be untied under tension by pulling on one end and capsizing the knot. It is unsuitable for joining ropes together, but if used to do so, the ropes must be of equal size and type otherwise it will slip.

A Reef Knot is formed with two overhand knots tied in opposite directions so that ends lie back alongside standing parts on their same sides.

*A Reef Knot fastening a bagged sail to the guardrail.*

*A Reef Knot securing a spinnaker pole to its deck chocks.*

# Slipped Reef Knot

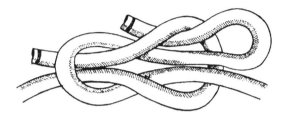

Formed in just the same way as a Reef Knot, but with one end doubled through to look like half a bow (look at your shoe laces). The advantage comes when trying to undo the knot if it has worked up very tight. The doubled end can then be given a good, hard pull and the first overhand knot falls undone. The load will then release the second part. It's very good if your fingers are cold and numb.

# Figure of Eight

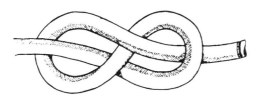

This knot looks just like its name – a number 8. It is a stopper knot formed in the free end of a rope to prevent its running out through a block, sheave or fairlead. Thus it is generally used in halyard falls, sheet ends, reefing lines, kicking straps and so on.

It is used in preference to an overhand knot by seamen as it is bulkier, thus preventing the line running out through larger holes, and it does not bind so tightly, making it easier to undo when required.

*Figure of Eight used in the end of a genoa sheet.*

# Bowline

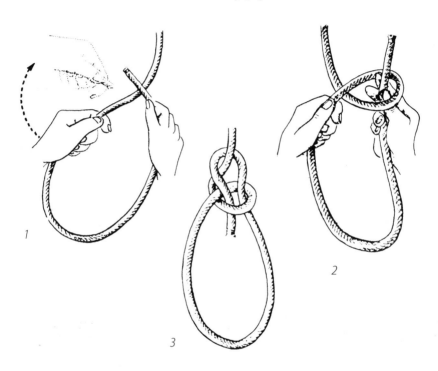

*1*

*2*

*3*

Probably the most useful knot on a boat, the Bowline provides a standing loop in the end of a line. Easy to tie, the knot is also easy to undo even after being under severe load.

There are many ways to tie a Bowline and the end can lie inside or outside the final loop. The easiest way in light line is to apply the end of the line to the standing part, and twist as shown so that it appears through a loop. Then pass round the standing part and back down through the initial loop. This process is a knack, but easily learned.

The Bowline must be worked up tight, particularly in springy synthetic ropes.

# Round Turn and Two Half Hitches

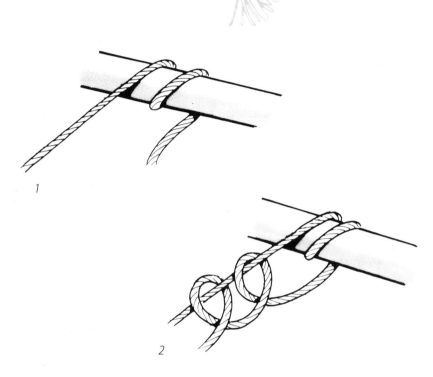

1

2

Usually used to secure a line to a spar, eye or ring, the Hitch is formed by passing the line round the spar (for example) in a complete round turn – so that the spar is completely enclosed by the rope and the working end is pointing back down the standing part – then tying what amounts to a Clove Hitch (see page 12) about the standing part. The working end passes round the standing part, crosses itself away from the original Round Turn and goes round again in a second Hitch as can be seen in the photographs.

Common uses include securing fenders to grabrails or stanchions, painters to towing eyes on dinghies or mooring rings on quaysides.

# Fisherman's Bend or Anchor Bend

This is very similar in formation to the Round Turn and Two Half Hitches, but is somewhat more secure. As can be seen the working end of the line passes under the Round Turn on the anchor ring so that it is locked under load. The Half Hitches are then put on in the same way as for the Round Turn and Two Half Hitches. Finally the rope's end, for complete security, can either be seized to the standing part as in the photograph or linked to it with a Bowline.

# Clove Hitch

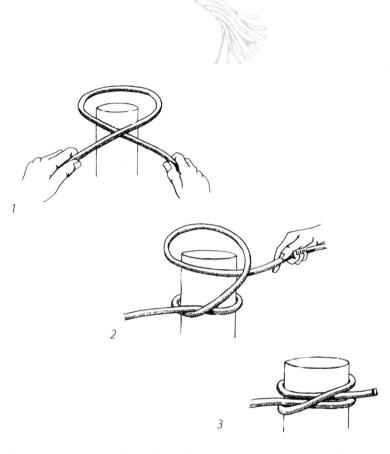

1

2

3

This is a much misused knot. Equal loads (or at least nearly equal) must be applied continuously to both sides otherwise it will roll and eventually undo. Therefore it should *not* be used to moor a boat as all the load will be on one side and the boat will, sooner or later, be lost.

To form the Hitch, the working end is either passed round and round the object the line is being hitched to or, if the top is open, preformed loops are dropped over as shown. This method is easier but not always possible. With laid rope, form loops by twisting *with* the lay.

Above: Clove Hitch used to lash the tiller amidships.

Left: Clove Hitches used to tie halyards off the mast.

# Lighterman's Hitch

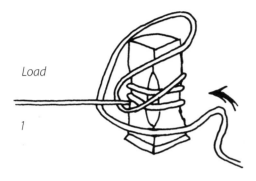

Load

1

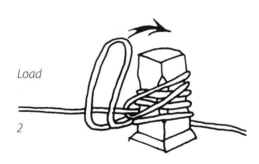

Load

2

This Hitch, also called a Tugboat Hitch and a 'No-name Knot', is particularly useful when taking a tow as it can be released under even the greatest tension. To form, take a round turn on the samson post then pass a bight under the standing part and drop it down over the top of the post. Take another turn (not a round turn) on the post then again pass a bight under the standing part and drop it down over the post. This process can be repeated as often as required to prevent slipping under load.

# Sheet Bend or Becket Bend

*Sheet Bend*

A Sheet Bend is used to join two lines together and is referred to as a Becket Bend when one rope has an eye already spliced in the end.

Where a standing eye does not exist a bight is taken in the end of one line (usually the thicker line) and the end of the other line is passed through it, round the back of the two standing parts and across the eye by threading under itself. The diagram should make this clear, but do take care to finish with the working ends of the two lines on the same side. And pull it tight.

*Above: Sheet Bend. Below: Becket Bend.*

# Double Sheet or Becket Bend

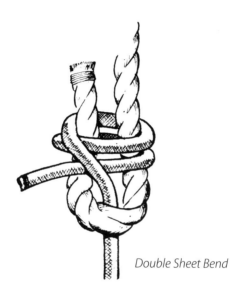

*Double Sheet Bend*

For added security a Sheet or Becket Bend (previous page) can quickly be transformed into a Double Bend by taking the working end of line round behind the standing loop and across parallel to itself for a second time.

The Double Bend is inevitably slightly slower to form but is much more secure in slippery or springy synthetic fibre ropes, having far less tendency to fall apart when not under load.

*Above: Double Sheet Bend. Below: Double Becket Bend.*

# Rolling Hitch on Rope

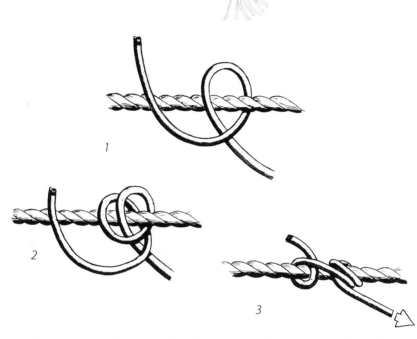

*1*

*2*

*3*

Used to secure one line to another, for example a line being used to relieve tension on another, the Rolling Hitch remains most secure when load is applied from a direction roughly parallel to the standing rope.

The Hitch is formed by taking a turn about the standing rope followed by a second crossing over itself. This immediately locks the line and a final Half Hitch finishes the whole thing off. Greatest security is achieved if the turns are put on *with* the lay of the standing rope.

Occasionally a very stiff or springy synthetic rope will not remain secure when formed into a Rolling Hitch. It slips simply because the turns cannot grip properly. In this case a third initial turn should be taken to help bind the rope to either spar or second rope.

# Rolling Hitch About a Spar

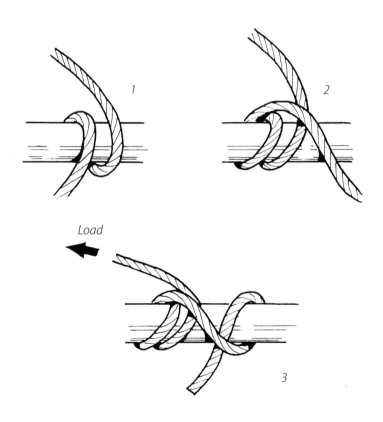

Load

1

2

3

A slightly different form of Rolling Hitch from the basic one described already is used when securing a rope to a spar rather than to another rope. In this case the initial turns do not cross over each other, they simply roll around the spar. The final Half Hitch is still formed beyond the point where the standing part of the line meets the spar.

# Figure of Eight Loop

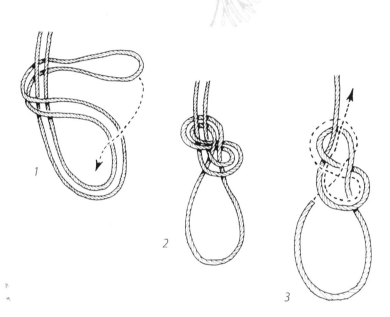

While a Bowline suits almost all purposes where a loop is required, it may not hold in very hard, slippery synthetics and can well be replaced by the Figure of Eight Loop. This is often also used where a loop is required midway along a rope as it is quicker to form than a Bowline on the bight. In this situation a simple Figure of Eight knot is tied with a bight of the rope rather than the bitter end (1 and 2).

Where it has to be tied through an eye or ring, or about an object that a loop cannot be slipped over, the method shown in 3 is used. Tie a Figure of Eight with a long working end and then 'double' it in the reverse direction with the ring or eye enclosed by a suitable loop in the working end. Both processes result in identical knots.

# Constrictor Knot

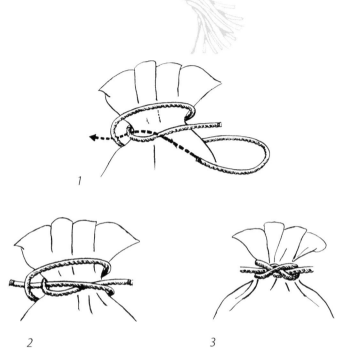

1

2                                              3

Originated by Clifford W Ashley, author of the famous *Ashley Book of Knots*, the Constrictor can well be used as a temporary whipping or seizing. It may also serve to tie the neck of a sailbag or kit bag, but in this case a slipped version might be desirable to make eventual undoing easier.

The essence of the knot is that it becomes ever tighter as tension is applied to the ends without loosening as the strain is taken off them.

To form the knot, take a Round Turn with the working end crossing the standing part (like the beginning of a Rolling Hitch) and make an overhand knot beneath the crossover point using the working end and the standing part. This process should be made clear by the diagrams. Then pull as tight as required. For easier untying, form a slipped overhand knot using a bight in the working end.

# Surgeon's Knot

This might be described as the Reef Knot for springy or slippery synthetics as it performs the same task but is more secure in modern materials. There are two forms; the more established is formed in the same way as a Reef Knot but with a second turn at each stage. Thus the square knot becomes a rectangle as shown in the diagram.

The second form has two initial overhand knots again, but instead of a second pair on top there is just one. Then, when the knot is drawn up tight the upper overhand knot forms a parallel crossover leaving the ends sticking out on opposite sides. It is not so neat, but when drawn up tightly does form a very secure, locked knot. The photographs show the differences.

*Standard Surgeon's Knot.*

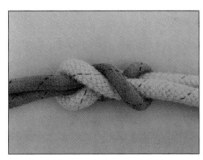

*Alternative Surgeon's Knot.*

# Carrick Bend

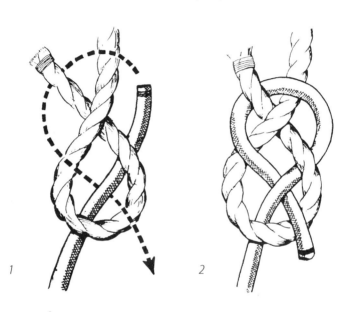

1                            2

This is an excellent knot for joining two lines together, whatever their material or relative diameters and is often used for adding an extra line to a kedge warp.

A loop is made in the end of one line with the working end crossing the standing part. The working end of the other line is then laid across and underneath the loop, passed over the first line's standing part, under its working end, over the first part of the original loop, under itself and over the other side of the original loop. Thus it has been woven alternately over and under each part as shown in the diagrams. When drawn tight the knot capsizes leaving the bitter ends together and parallel.

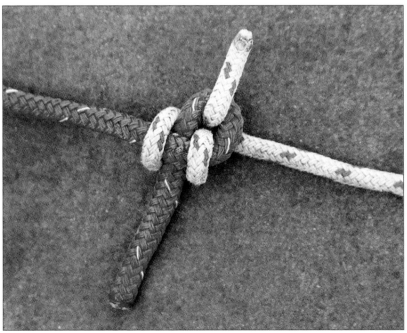

# Sheepshank

Commonly described as a knot for shortening a line temporarily, the Sheepshank has more practical value as a means of bypassing a chafed section of rope (see bottom photo on opposite page).

Where this is the intention, a bight is taken in the line well to one side of the damaged area and brought back alongside the standing part on the other side of the damage. There it is applied to the standing part and twisted, as in the Bowline or Waggoner's Hitch, to leave the bight protruding through a loop in the standing part. The remaining bight is applied to the standing part next to it in the same way. The result is a Sheepshank as shown with the chafed rope in the middle. If formed correctly this can actually be cut through without the knot falling apart so long as tension is maintained. To prevent the Sheepshank falling apart when not under load, seize the 'ears' to the standing parts as shown.

# Marling Hitch

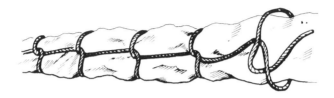

A series of Marling Hitches can be used to lash a sail to its boom or yard or to secure a bundle of sail to a guardrail or to the boom.

Each of the series of Hitches is formed by passing the line down around the sail bundle (for example), up over the part lying along the sail and then tucked down under itself in a direction on along the bundle of sail. The diagram and photograph show this. Instead of tucking the working end down under itself it may just as well be tucked upwards. In both cases the effect is a chain of overhand knots spaced out along the sail.

# Waggoner's or Trucker's Hitch

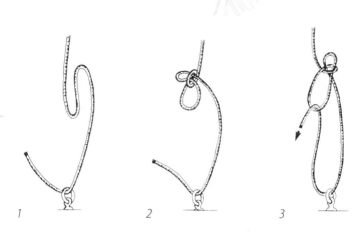

1        2        3

Widely used for lashing down loads on lorries, this Hitch gives a 2:1 purchase without the use of blocks or other devices. It's simple to form and falls apart when the strain is taken off it.

The line is first passed through a strong eye or under a securing hook. Two parallel bights are formed above the strong point, one upward and one downward. The upward one is applied to the standing part and twisted as though forming a Bowline so that the bight protrudes through a loop. The working end is then passed through the other (downward) bight and tension is applied to tighten the whole lashing.

*Waggoner's Hitch in use.*

# Buntline Fisherman's Bend

This is an adaptation of a Fisherman's Bend particularly well suited to use with slippery synthetics.

The first round turn is as described for a Fisherman's Bend with the working end passing under the round turn. Then the working end is passed round the standing part and is used to form a Clove Hitch *towards* the anchor ring (or whatever) and is worked up tight.

# Spar Hitch

This is something of a cross between a Clove Hitch and a Constrictor Knot. It grips better than a Clove Hitch where there is greater load on one side than the other, but is more easily undone than a Constrictor. To make the Spar Hitch a turn is taken around the spar with the working end crossing over the standing part before going round again. It then crosses over itself and tucks under the standing part. All that remains is to work the knot tight.

# Sliding Figures of Eight

This simple bend provides the same services as a Carrick Bend in that it securely joins two lines of unequal thickness and remains easy to undo.

The working ends of each rope are laid side by side in opposite directions. Each is then used to form a Figure of Eight knot about the standing part of its sister rope, the latter being enclosed by one turn of the Figure of Eight (it doesn't matter which). These knots are worked tight and slid together. To undo the knot the bitter ends are simply pulled apart to slide the knots apart allowing them to be undone.

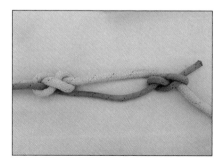

# Stopper

This is hardly a knot at all, relying essentially on friction rather than on binding. It is mostly used when relieving the load on one line by attaching another, such as when trying to undo a riding turn on a winch or sharing the load on a mooring cable.

A turn is taken with the relieving line's working end so that it crosses over itself (as in the first photograph). The end is then rolled on around the loaded cable for several turns before either being held by hand or half hitched to the cable. Load is then applied to the relieving line. The Stopper Knot can be undone even under load by releasing the bitter end and casting off the turns.

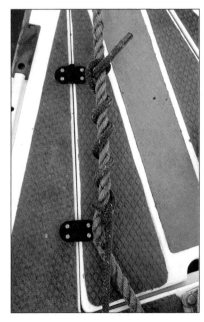

# Bowline on the Bight

 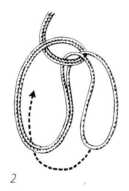 

1                     2                     3

This is a good way of providing a loop in the middle of a line or for making an emergency bosun's chair. It's not comfortable to sit in but it does work.

To form a Bowline on the Bight take a bight of the line, apply it to the standing part and twist in the normal manner resulting in its sticking up through a turn of the standing part. The protruding 'ear' is pulled through, spread out and dropped over the two part main loop. It is brought up above the turn of the standing part and settled down. It then looks just like a doubled Bowline but without the usual end inside the main loop.

# Spanish Bowline

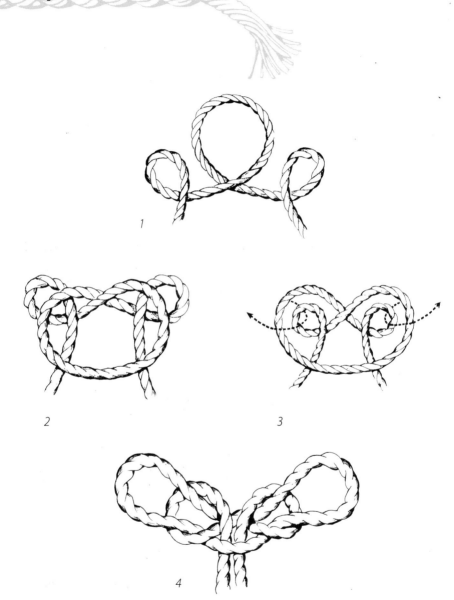

1

2

3

4

The Spanish Bowline, like the Bowline on the Bight, produces two loops enabling it to be used as a substitute bosun's chair or perhaps for slinging a ladder or plank over the side to form a paint staging.

Spanish Bowline's formation is unlike a true Bowline and is a bit complicated. Centre the rope and lay it out in three loops as in the first diagram. Fold the middle, large loop down, spread it out to enclose the two smaller loops and pull bights of the large loop up through each of the small ones, pulling them through as a pair of 'ears'. Settle the whole knot tightly.

*Above left: substitute for a bosun's chair with one leg through each loop.*
*Above right: substitute for a bosun's chair, sitting in one loop while a second loop supports the back.*

# Jury or Masthead Knot

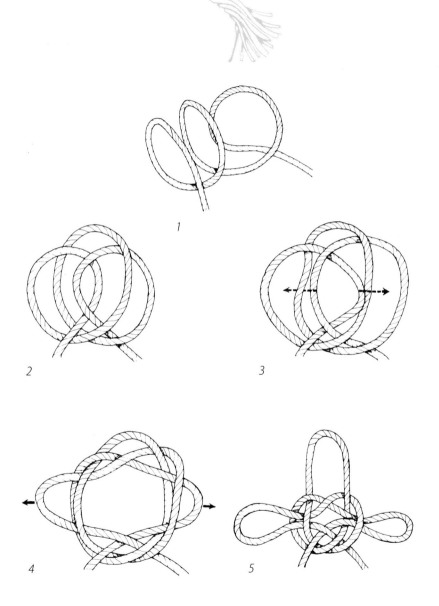

1

2

3

4

5

A Masthead Knot may be used for attaching shrouds to a jury mast or for erecting a temporary flag pole and many other similar applications.

Three loops are formed and interleaved so that the left part of the bottom one overlaps the right side of the top one in the centre of the middle loop. These two sides are then pulled out in a weaving pattern as shown and the top side of the middle loop is pulled upward. The process produces three loops and two tails, which can be linked to form another loop. The masthead or pole top inserts in the centre of the whole knot. Guys or shrouds are then attached to the knot's loops with Becket Bends.

# Hunter's Bend

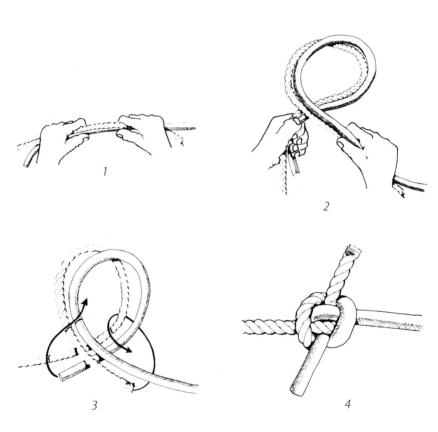

1

2

3

4

Used for joining two ropes together, the Hunter's Bend is well suited to stiff or slippery synthetic ropes. It is a square shaped knot formed by laying the two working ends parallel, but pointing in opposite directions, then forming them into a loop, and turning the working ends through the loop. The bend is then worked tight.

# Coiling Hitches

# Halyard Coil

Halyard falls should always be coiled up and tidied off the deck as quickly as possible; otherwise they become tangled up possibly causing serious trouble. The easiest and simplest way is to make a neat coil beginning at the cleat and working towards the free end. Always coil *with* the lay of the rope if it is a laid rope, or in figures of eight if it's plaited as shown here. Once the line is coiled, hold it in the left hand, reach through the coils with your right hand and grasp the line near the cleat. Pull a bight back through the coils, twist it and slip it over the upper horn of the cleat, either directly or by passing it behind the standing part of the halyard for additional security.

# Half Hitch Coil for Stowage

A line that is to be coiled up and stowed away must be 'tied' in some way to stop it uncoiling. The quickest way is to coil the rope and then, using a working end, form a loop as shown, lead the end over the top of the coils and back underneath to emerge through the small loop. Pull up tight in a Half Hitch. The coil will remain secure if the working end is used to hang it on a hook in the locker or some other securing point so that the weight keeps tension on the Half Hitch.

# Buntline or Gasket Coil

More secure than the Half Hitch Coil, the Buntline Coil can either be hung up or simply laid down in a locker without coming undone. Coil up the rope in the usual manner but leave a long tail. Pass this working end round and round the coils (in an upward direction) to bind them together. Then push a bight through the top of the coils. Lift it up and spread it out so that it can drop down over the coils to lie at the top of the frapping turns. All is then worked tight and the fall may be used to hang the coil up. The Gasket Coil can also (as it was originally) be used to tidy up a fixed line in situ as shown in the photograph overleaf.

# 2

# Whippings

The basic purpose of whipping a rope's end is to prevent it fraying or unlaying, which is a waste; it also ensures that the rope will pass easily through blocks and eyes.

# Common Whipping

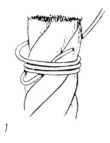

1

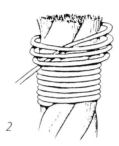

2

3

Not the securest of whippings, the Common is nevertheless adequate for most purposes. The basic method is to lay the end of the whipping twine along the rope (towards the rope's bitter end) and pass turns tightly over it to anchor it and cover it. Apply further turns, leaving the last few loose so that the end of the twine can be tucked back under them before they are worked tight to hold it in place. Cut off flush any excess of twine.

Alternatively, begin with a loop of twine laid along the rope. Apply turns over it as far as required and then pass the end of the twine through the loop, which is then drawn down into the centre of the whipping. Cut both ends off flush.

# West Country Whipping

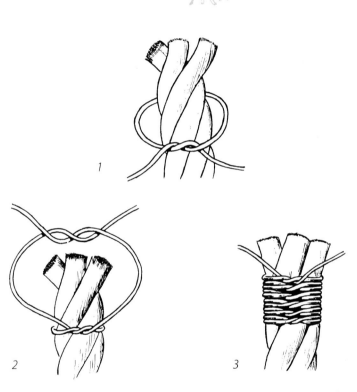

1

2

3

This is a more secure whipping than the straightforward Common Whipping but is a little slower to apply. Form a series of overhand knots on alternate sides of the rope; that is one at the front, next at the back, then at the front again and so on. When sufficient whipping has been applied, finish off with a Reef Knot (see page 2).

For further security in addition to using waxed whipping twine, give each overhand knot a second tuck (as for a Surgeon's Knot, page 27).

# Needle and Palm Whipping

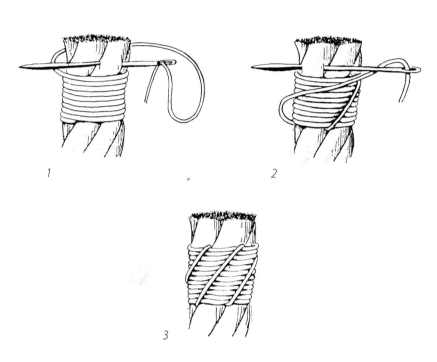

*1*

*2*

*3*

This is one of the most secure of the widely used whippings as it is actually sewn onto the rope with a needle and palm. Begin as though making a Common Whipping and, when sufficient turns have been put on, thread the twine through the eye of a needle. Stitch through one strand of the rope and worm the twine back down the lay of the rope over the whipping turns. Stitch through into the next groove and worm upwards. Stitch through again and worm down. Repeat, stitching and worming down until all have been doubled. Finish with several stitches through the rope.

# Sailmaker's Whipping

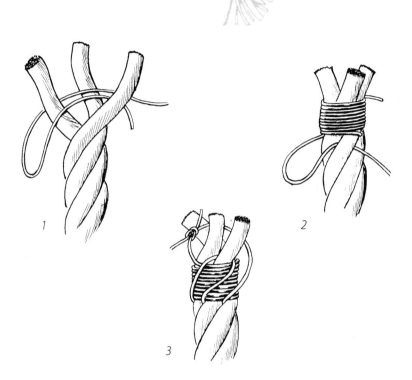

The Sailmaker's Whipping looks exactly like a needle and palm one but is not actually stitched to the rope, the worming parts passing behind each strand. To begin, a loop of whipping twine is passed round a strand of the unlaid rope's end, which is then laid up to include the twine. The rope's end is then whipped with the twine. The original loop is dropped over the end of the strand it was formed round and pulled tight using the end protruding beneath the whipping. This end is then wormed up to the top of the whipping and tied off to the other end of the twine with a Reef or Surgeon's Knot.

# Alternatives to Whipping

A very quick, temporary measure to stop a rope's end fraying further is to bind it with adhesive tape. It is surprisingly effective but must be regarded solely as a stop gap measure.

A very tidy modern method of finishing an end is to fit a heat shrink plastic sleeve. These sleeves fit loosely over the rope's end until they are heated in a flame. The heat shrinks the plastic so that the sleeve grips tightly onto the rope.

Perhaps the commonest way to deal with a synthetic rope's end these days is to melt it in a flame so that the fibres seal together. A neat end is not all that easy to achieve as it must be moulded into shape without allowing it to stick to and burn your fingers. Try binding the end with paper, cutting through to neaten it and then putting it in a flame with the paper holding the strands together. Alternatively, melt the end, well wet your fingers and pinch it into shape. A hot knife blade may also be used.

*Alternatives to whipping the end of a rope include the use of electrician's tape, heat sealing, and heat shrink sleeves.*

# 3

# Splicing

# Short Splice

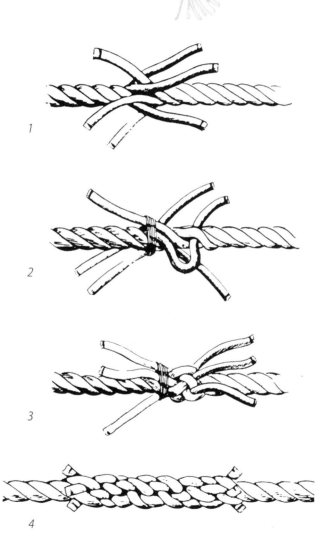

1

2

3

4

Several knots can be used for joining ropes together, but none is as strong as a Short Splice. It can cause problems by increasing the diameter of the line making it unlikely to render through blocks and where this is important a Long Splice must be used. To form a Short Splice the ends of each part to be joined are unlaid and the ends of each strand stopped with tape, or whipping twine – use a Constrictor Knot. The strands of each part are then married and one set of strands stopped to the other rope with tape (or Constrictor). The free strands are then alternately tucked against the lay into the other rope in an over and under pattern. The stopped strands are then freed and the same process is carried out on that side. After three or four tucks each side, cut off the excess of each strand leaving protruding ends. This allows the splice to settle without untucking. Roll splice underfoot to help settle it.

*Short splice (above) used to repair rope damage (right).*

# Long Splice

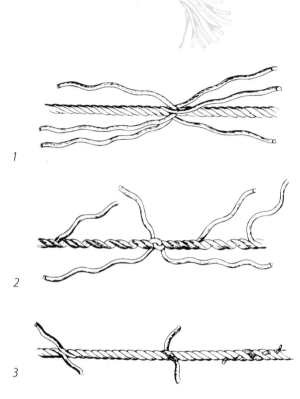

1

2

3

A Long Splice hardly increases a rope's diameter but is a little less strong than a Short Splice. It can be formed in many different ways, but this is a widely used method. Each line is unlaid for some distance (about ten turns) and the strands married. One strand each side is unlaid a further distance (about six turns) and its opposite number laid up in its place. Thus the line should always look like a complete piece of laid rope. Each of the three pairs of strands spread along the rope is now knotted to its neighbour with an overhand knot before being thinned with a sharp knife and tucked (over and under) against the lay of the rope. Again rolling underfoot will help to settle the splice.

# Three Strand Eye Splice

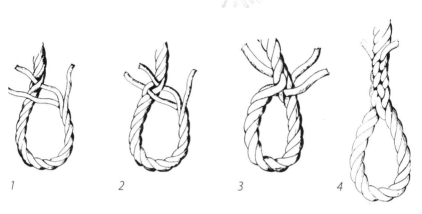

1          2          3          4

An Eye Splice provides the strongest and most permanent eye or loop in the end of a rope. Unlay the strands a short distance and seal or temporarily whip their ends. Tuck the middle strand under one strand of the standing part, against the rope's lay, at the point where you require the throat of the splice. The strand now lying on the inside of the eye is tucked into the next strand at the same point, followed by the third strand under the remaining strand at the back of the standing part. All tucks should be at the same point on the standing part. Next make three or four further tucks against the lay with each strand in turn. Cut off the ends; not too short, and preferably do not whip them unless appearance matters. Roll splice underfoot to settle.

# Multiplait Eye Splice

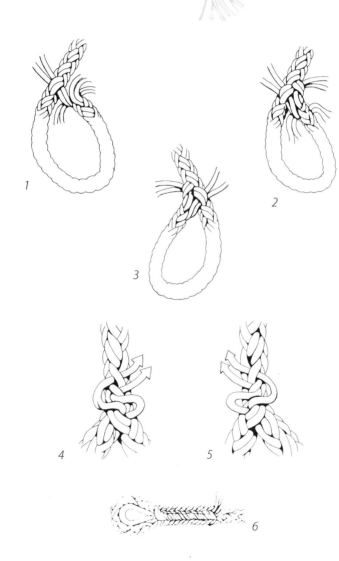

1

2

3

4

5

6

Multiplait rope comprises a plait of pairs of right- and left-hand strands. Right-hand strands have black marker thread. Form an eye to the right of the standing part, unplait and tuck a pair of right-handed strands under a convenient right-handed pair in the standing part. Tuck the adjacent left-handed pair under the adjacent left-handed pair in the standing part. Turn the splice over and repeat as above, using the remaining two pairs. Now separate the strands and tuck individually using the same sets of strands to give a characteristic 'parallel' appearance to the splice. Complete five tucks; finally, whip strands in pairs.

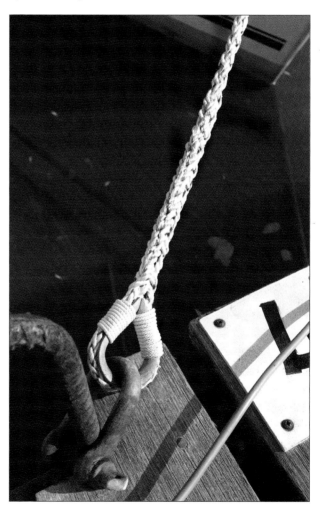

# Stitch and Whip Eye in Plaited Rope

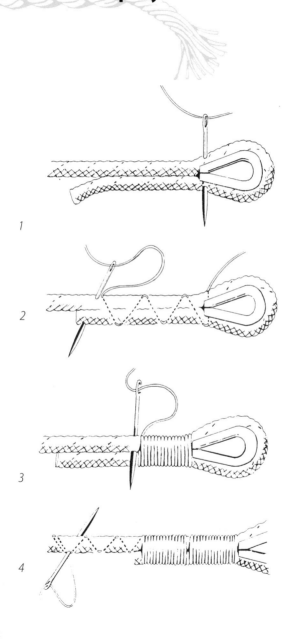

1

2

3

4

Not as strong as an Eye Splice, but plaited rope is almost impossible to splice, so it must suffice. Form an eye as required with at least 3 in (75 mm) tail measured from the throat. Using waxed twine stitch back and forth from the throat to the end and back. Cut the thread, and hammer the rope parts together. Now whip from the throat and hammer tight after a few turns. Halfway through whipping stitch through rope to lock the whipping. Continue to end and finish with several stitches through the standing part of the rope.

# Laid Core Eye Splice

This splice requires a long needle-like fid. Begin by forming a tight overhand loop knot 2m from the rope's end to bind core and sheath together, then measure about 250 mm back from the rope's end and make mark A.

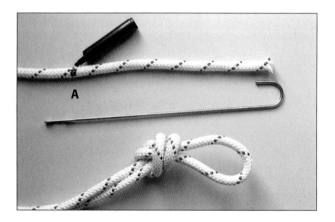

Form the size of eye required and make mark B at the throat against A.

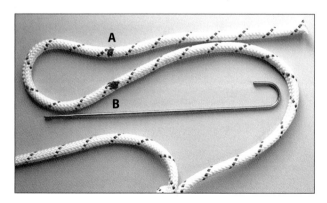

Open the sheath at B (using an ordinary fid) and extract the core, then tape round it alongside mark A.

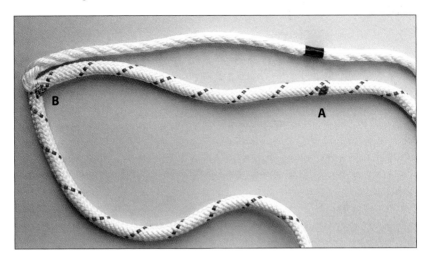

Unlay the core back to this tape and cut off half of one strand and three-quarters of another. Bind the end of each strand tightly with tape before taping the three strands together. (It's not easy to get the tape on tightly as the core fibres spring apart very readily, but the bindings must be tight enough to slide into the sheath in the next step.)

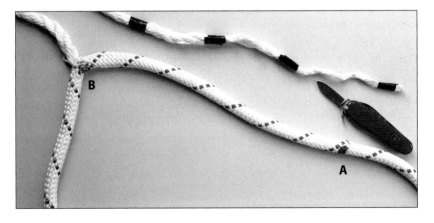

Insert the needle into the cover through the throat at B and out at A. Thread the end of the core into the needle's eye and pull the core through the sheath and out at B. Insert a thimble if required, milk the sheath, and pull the core to settle them round the eye and thimble.

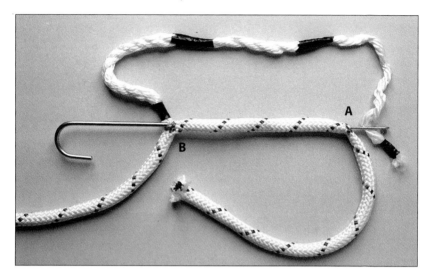

Untape the core and lay the three strands alongside the rope. Insert the needle into the sheath just short of the longest strand, exiting at the throat of the splice (B). Use the needle to pull the longest strand of core through and out of the side of the sheath. Repeat with each of the shortened strands.

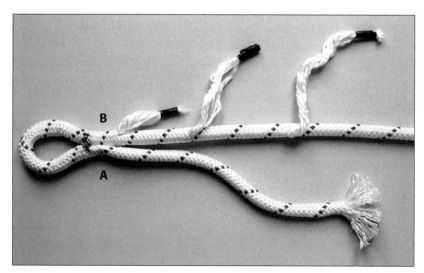

Tug on their exposed ends to tighten the eye. Cut the ends off close and milk the sheath to hide them.

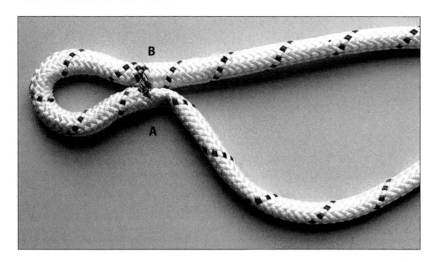

There are two ways to finish off. Either, unbraid the empty tail of sheath back to the throat and pull individual strands (or small groups of strands) down under the main part of the sheath below the throat, just like the three core strands. Spread these strands around the rope and cut them to random lengths, milking the sheath to hide their ends. This is a very tedious and often extremely difficult operation (because of the quantity of material crowding in below the throat), but gives a neat, tidy and very secure result. Or, if you can't manage that process, cut the length of the sheath down and cover it with a tight whipping like that on page 62.

# Braid on Braid Eye Splice

Braid on braid is perhaps the most widely used rope construction and although this eye splice appears complicated, it can retain around 85 per cent of the rope's strength. A purpose-made tubular fid is essential.

First make a tight overhand or figure of eight loop knot 3m from the rope's end to bind core and sheath together. Next make mark A one fid length back from the rope's end (using a felt tip marker), form the required size of eye and mark B across the throat from A.

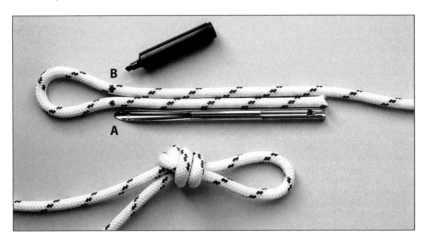

Use the tip of the fid to open the sheath at B and mark the exposed core C.

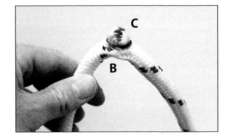

Now pull the core out so that it is free of the sheath, pull the sheath further back and make mark D one fid length on from C; make mark E two thirds of a fid from D.

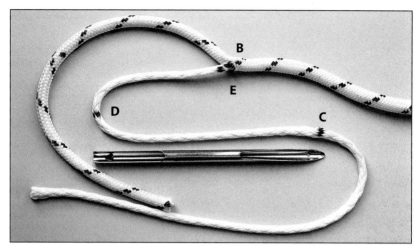

Push the end of the sheath into the hollow fid, making sure it catches on the built-in hook, insert the fid at D, push it gently through the centre of the core and pull it out at E. Unhook the fid and pull the sheath back into the core so its end is just hidden.

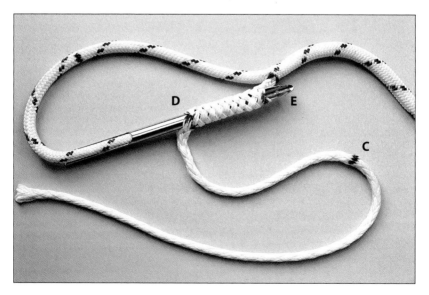

Fix the end of the core into the fid, insert it into the sheath at mark A and pull it out just past B.

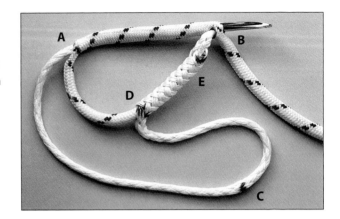

Run your hands up the rope from the knot, milking the sheath towards the eye and also round the eye from B towards A, so that core and sheath settle into each other.

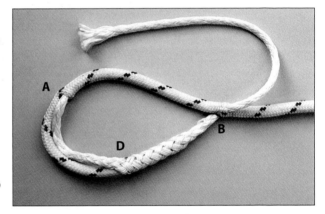

With everything settled into place, pull a short length of the core out again and cut the free part off, then milk round the splice to hide the shortened end. Hook the eye over a strong point and give the whole splice a hard tug to settle it down.

# High Tech, Low Stretch

Materials and construction techniques have come a long way in recent years and continue to be developed at amazing rates, driven by the high performance requirements of offshore and trans-ocean high budget racers. Unfortunately, though some of the more exotic materials really are very expensive indeed; for the most part high performance comes at an acceptable price.

   The main benefits of these high tech lines are their light weight coupled with high strength and low stretch. Indeed, for the majority of jobs on an average boat, strength is not something we need to worry about. If the line is thick enough for easy handling, it's strong enough for the job. (This assumes sheaves of at least 5:1 diameter ratio and no kinks or sharp bends and careful knotting.) The questions to be asked then revolve around the degree of stretch that is either required or is acceptable, and the preferred construction. However, one thing that must be remembered on the matter of strength is that should a permanent eye be needed in the end of a line (for example, to fit a shackle on a halyard) that eye should be spliced in, not formed with a knot. A good splice will retain over 80 per cent of the rope's strength, but a knot will reduce the strength by up to 50 per cent. Frightening, isn't it?

## Materials and properties

**Polyester**, sometimes referred to by the abbreviation PES, is available as a three strand laid rope, a plait, a laid core with plaited sheath, or as a braid on braid line. Finishes can either be smooth or slightly roughened for easier handling. It's an excellent all round material for low stretch purposes such as halyards and sheets on dinghies and cruisers, where it's both durable and relatively chafe and chemical resistant. It's far from being the lowest stretch material available (25 per cent at break) nor is it the strongest (8g per denier), but for the average boatowner it represents good value for money in addition to being easy to handle and work.

**Nylon** (a contraction of New York and London, the two cities in which it was developed), has similar strength to polyester, but is stretchier (35 per cent extension at break). This made it popular for anchor rodes and mooring warps, but exposure to ultraviolet light and sea water (or at least the contaminants in sea water) rapidly discolour it and stiffen it, making it awkward to handle. For that reason, its popularity is waning and many people are changing to polyester; however you should avoid pre-stretched polyester in situations where you would previously have chosen nylon for its stretchiness. Nylon is available in three strand form as well as the special eight strand anchorbraid.

**Polypropylene**, sometimes shortened to PP, is usually considered cheap and cheerful, being at the bottom of the rope price range and available in several colours – though if you look at the current range of braided rope colours this may not be so remarkable as when it was first marketed. Polypropylene feels quite hard when handled and the smooth versions are quite slippery. Staple spun polypropylene has a 'hairy' finish, which gives a better (if not comfortable) grip. PP lines are not particularly strong when compared to other synthetics, but they are light and float, making them useful for lines on life-saving devices, but a menace to propellers.

**Kevlar®**, a trade name of Du Pont, is an aramid and was the first 'exotic' material used in rope making. It is light and almost three times as strong as polyester, but it is expensive and has proven to have poor durability in marine applications, being vulnerable to both ultraviolet light and abrasion. Kevlar® has largely been phased out by rope makers in favour of more recently developed materials.

**Dyneema®** is the trade name of DSM High Performance Fibers, and **Spectra®** is the trade name of Allied Fibers; so far as the yachtsman is concerned, these two high modulus polyethylene fibres are the same. They are the material of choice for high performance racing craft, having high strength (35g per denier, or more than four times that of polyester) and low stretch (only 3.5 per cent at break), but are very expensive. The high cost, though, is outweighed on these boats by the benefits of Dyneema® and

Spectra®, which include durability and resistance to ultraviolet light. They are always made up into core and sheath-style lines, and are usually spliced by rigging experts rather than simple seamen as it's a tricky process.

**Liquid Crystal Polymer Fibre (LCP)**, often referred to as **Vectran**® (a trade mark of Celanese), is a beautiful gold-coloured material that costs about as much as gold. It's light, only stretches 3.3 per cent at break, has high resistance to temperature, but is only moderately abrasion resistant. It is so affected by ultraviolet light that it is stored away from all daylight prior to being incorporated into a rope's core. It's three times as strong as polyester, which is rather less than Dyneema® or Spectra®, and costs (currently) around 20 times as much.

**PBO** (polyphenylene-2, 6-bezobisoxazole), or **Zylon**® (a trade mark of Toyobo Co), is the top of the range of the exotics. It is over five times as strong as polyester with 3.5 per cent extension at break, but it hates ultraviolet light and chemicals, although it doesn't mind heat. It costs a staggering 35 times as much as polyester at present, thus putting it into the realms of fantasy for most sailors.

## Knots knock strength

This is a fact far less widely recognized than it should be. Any knot will seriously reduce the strength of the line it is formed in, and to demonstrate this English Braids carried out a short series of tests exclusively for this book.

### TABLE OF STRENGTHS

| DIAMETER (MM) | BREAKING LOADS IN KG | | | | |
|---|---|---|---|---|---|
| | 6 | 8 | 10 | 12 | 14 |
| Braid on Braid | 1230 | 2000 | 2550 | 4000 | 6000 |
| Dyneema® | 1800 | 3200 | 4200 | 5700 | 7800 |
| Sixteen Plait Matt Polyester | 600 | 1460 | 1580 | 3400 | 4350 |
| Three Strand Polyester | | 1700 | 2340 | 3310 | 4180 |
| Three Strand Nylon | 780 | 1800 | 2800 | 3100 | 4900 |
| Eight Strand Anchorbraid | | 1400 | 2400 | 3000 | 3800 |
| Three Strand Polypropylene | 480 | 960 | 1430 | 2030 | 2790 |

It was found that a Bowline reduced the strength of a line by 30 per cent, a Figure of Eight loop by 28 per cent, and a Reef Knot by 50 per cent. Considering the number of occasions in which we use these knots on board our boats, these are pretty serious numbers, and should be borne in mind when selecting both ropes and knots for particular jobs.

## Right for the job

Even though knots do seriously reduce the ultimate strength of all ropes, it remains true to say that while we cannot ignore a rope's breaking strength, it is generally more important to select the right material for a particular use, coupled with a comfortable diameter for handling. If the material is right and you select a diameter that's easy to handle, the strength will be adequate.

### Sheets and halyards

The most popular choices for sheets and halyards are either braid on braid lines or sixteen plait polyester, which has a roughened surface that is very good to handle and grips well on winch barrels. The braid on braid needs to suffer a little bit of surface abrasion before it loses its superficial gloss and becomes as pleasant to handle as the sixteen plait. This is more apparent with sheets than halyards, and also, while sheets are commonly fastened to genoa clews with bowlines, halyards are shackled to the heads of sails, requiring an eye in the end of the halyard. It is far easier to make a good eye splice in braid on braid than the sixteen plait, making braid on braid the favoured choice for halyards. Incidentally, slight roughening of the cover on a braid on braid line does no real harm to the rope: it is the core that supplies the rope's strength.

On more performance orientated craft, Dyneema® or Spectra® ropes are growing in popularity, at least for halyards, as they stretch so little and maintain a good tight luff. In contrast, many 'traditional' (which usually means gaff rigged) boats are using buff coloured three strand polyester matt ropes as they are good to handle and look very much like old hemp or cotton lines.

### Anchoring and mooring

While many boatowners happily anchor using a good length of chain coupled with a nylon three strand laid rode, the eight plait anchor braids are a much better bet as they have been designed specifically for the job. These lines still require a generous length of chain cable next to the anchor to ensure a good horizontal pull and to take most of the abrasion on rough ground, but they are much less likely to snarl up and cannot twist into kinked knots as a laid rope twisted the wrong way will do. Like all plaited or braided ropes, these anchor braids should never be coiled in the neat loop associated with laid ropes: rather they must either be put into figures of eight or, better, flaked down in a series of back and forth runs, each layer at right angles to the lower one. Coiling a plaited rope will induce twist and it will snarl up as it tries to run out, whereas a laid rope needs to be twisted (in the direction of its lay) as it is coiled to ensure it does not tangle up. These two constructions produce lines with almost opposite properties in this respect.

An anchor braid will also have better 'give' characteristics for absorbing shock loads than a laid line will. When lying at anchor in strong winds and rough water, the shock loads on the rode and on the deck fittings can be substantial and the braided construction copes with these by virtue of the springiness of its construction as well as the elasticity of the nylon itself. A laid rope has far less constructional 'give'.

Capstans and windlasses should be able to cope equally well with either type of construction.

When it comes to mooring lines, it's common to see all sorts used – laid, braid on braid and anchor braid – in nylon, polypropylene or polyester. All too often they are offcuts from old headsail sheets that have seen better days. Though it's understandable that owners use such lines rather than just put them in the rubbish bin, it's not advisable. If the lines have reached the end of their working lives for one purpose, it's likely that they will be no better for another, especially the serious task of securing your valuable investment to the dock.

There are, of course, arguments in favour of each material – nylon, polyester, polypropylene – but, after cost, the thing to look for is ultraviolet resistance, since these are the lines that will be exposed to the sun for most time. It's a sad fact that the majority of boats spend far more time moored than at sea, so their docking lines are the most heavily used.

## Handling ropes and lines

Not surprisingly, some consideration has to be given to the handling and care of all these high tech ropes.

**Do**:
- Keep them coiled or hanked neatly to prevent tangling.
- Run them out carefully to avoid kinking and knotting.
- Coil laid ropes in clockwise loops (for right-hand lay) and use figures of eight for braids.
- Wash out salt, sand, grit and mud, which will otherwise chafe and destroy the fibres.
- Try to hang coiled or hanked ropes in a locker rather than dump them in an untidy heap.
- Protect all lines from chafe.
- Use eye splices rather than knotted loops for permanent or high load attachments.
- Use blocks whose sheaves have diameters in the ratio of at least 5:1 with that of the ropes they will carry.
- Ensure the rope fits comfortably into the groove of the sheave it's passing round.
- Seal and whip ropes' ends. Braided sheaths in particular fray very quickly.

**Don't**:
- Leave high tech lines exposed to high levels of ultraviolet light for long periods of time.
- Kink or twist any type of rope.
- Don't stand or walk on ropes and lines.
- Surge lines, particularly polypropylene ones, too fast around winches or cleats or they'll melt.
- Use rope stoppers that are likely to crush the rope's core; some of the more exotic materials are prone to damage of this nature.

*Well organized running rigging makes sailing safer and easier.*

# Flemish Wire Eye Splice

Suitable for wire *rope* (7 x 7 or 7 x 19) this way of making an eye requires no tucking and is therefore very easy, unlike most wire splicing.

Divide the rope's end into two parts; one of three strands, one of four including the straight core strand. Tape the ends, then unlay to at least four times the length of the eye. Cross one part over the other to form the eye.

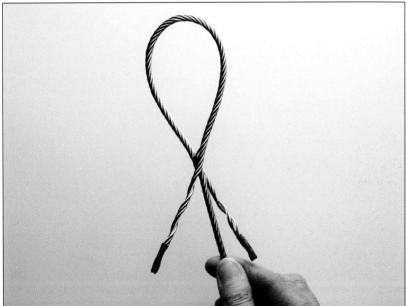

Take each part in turn and lay it into the empty groove down the opposite side of the eye to the throat.

Cut out the heart strand and, if required, insert thimble. Pull each part back to its own side and lay up together spiralling round the standing part.

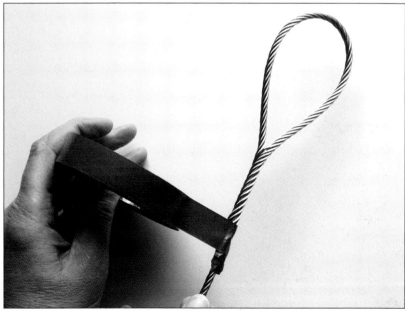

Serve over with tape.

# Multiplait to Chain Splice

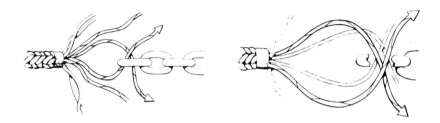

This splice allows a rope/chain junction to pass through a navel pipe or fair-lead. Unlay four pairs of strands for a distance equal to 12 chain links, and seize. Look straight at the heart of the rope: of four pairs of strands one lies at the top, one at the bottom and two are crossed in the middle (see photo overleaf). Use the crossed pair for your first tuck. Either both have black marker thread or both are plain. Separate the strands in each pair and tuck them through the first link, two from above and two from below.

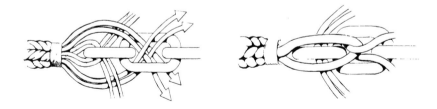

For the second tuck lead the strands along either side of the first link and tuck them crosswise through the second link.

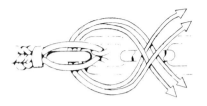

Pull tight to settle. Continue tucking with alternate pairs.

# Index